God Has *a* Smoking Jacket

and Other Poetic Musings

God Has *a* Smoking Jacket

and Other Poetic Musings

RICHARD H. BARRY

with Garrison Foxwaters and
Yusuf Ishqzoda

To request permissions, contact the publisher at permissions@rhb.pub.

Paperback: 979-8-9877572-3-9

Library of Congress Control Number: 2025910345

First edition August 2025.

Edited by Malia Mendez
Cover by Natalie Lauren Design

Excerpt from "The Only Sin I Know," from *I Heard God Laughing: Poems of Hope and Joy* by Daniel Ladinsky © 1996 & 2006, with permission. www.danielladinsky.com.

Excerpt from "Jerusalem," from *Love Poems from God: Twelve Sacred Voices from the East and West* by Daniel Ladinsky © 2002, with permission. www.danielladinsky.com.

Published by Richard H. Barry
Lisbon, New Hampshire
rbarry@rhb.pub

To Amanda, you know what you did

Contents

Overture

Contact

Climax

Afterglow

Overture

God Has a Smoking Jacket

God has a smoking jacket.

I first learned this
From a reputable source
Who ran into the Friend
At a lodge he hadn't visited
For quite some time.

And there was God,
Nestled equal parts
Into his merino wool wrapping
And an oversized armchair,
Elated at my source's
Much-hoped-for return,
Throwing his arms up,
Jubilantly exclaiming,
"You're back!"

Well,
Given that the Friend and I
Have been living together
For several years now—

And, upon his insistence,

Have absolutely zero boundaries—

I decided to verify my source's claim

By making the short trip down the hall

To investigate the contents of

God's closet.

Slinging its door open,

My left eyebrow

Slowly journeyed upward

As I took in the sight of a wardrobe

Not only including smoking jackets

But comprised almost entirely of them

And all other manner of shamelessly

Decadent loungewear.

I swear you've never seen

So many robes.

And. So. Much. Velvet.

An ungodly amount,

Which is rather ironic

For God.

And perched on the closet's lone shelf,

A mahogany valet,

In which were stored—

No joke—

Straight up monocles, fam.

At least a dozen of 'em.

What does it say to you

That God has a wardrobe

Like that?

It tells me he's living,

As Lady Underhill would put it,

In step with the Leisure of Eternity.

God Has a Label Maker

God has a label maker,
But it seems to be stuck
On the "Good" setting.

"Good," after all,
Is the only label I've ever found
Attached to her many creations.

God Has a Frying Pan

God has a frying pan.

I know this because I saw
Her initials etched into its handle
When she handed it to me yesterday,

Saying,

"Here,
You take over for a while.
I need a break!"

Naturally, I asked,

"God, why do you have a frying pan,
And what am I supposed to do with it?"

"The same thing I do,"

She stated matter-of-factly,

"Use it to knock some sense
Into anyone who suggests

That life with me
Is anything other
Than a Dance."

Something God Doesn't Have

How many ways
Can I make the
Same point?

This time I'll try
An outright command.

You are hereby ordered
To cease and desist
Fretting over whether or not
You're on God's bad side.

It's impossible, after all,
To get on something
God doesn't have.

Holy Voltage

I am an atom-thick tungsten wire
By which our 1.21-gigawatt God
Is constantly trying
To light up the world.

Only so much Holy Voltage can be conducted—
And we're quickly running out of fuses!

That's why the countless filaments
Of souls on this sacred blue dot—
That's why you and I—
So sorely need one another.

We are designed, even destined,
To be braided,
To be spun into an incandescent,
Indestructible Fabric,
Charged and glowing
From the act of
God making love.

Such effulgent sheets
Won't light up just the world
But every corner of existence.

Curious Species

We humans sure are
A curious species
With exceedingly
Peculiar habits.

I can't imagine
Any other creature
Spending even half
As much time
Trying to get
What it already has.

Most Just Borrow Words

Few are the initiated,

Few are the Divine's
True Lovers,

For most don't have the courage
To undress before God.

Most just borrow words
From those brave souls
Who've dared Consent
To the Amorous One's
Endlessly inventive,
Relentlessly seductive
Glances.

Someone has stolen the
Lexicon of Love,

Some imposter got his hands on
A copy of God's *Kama Sutra*,

And has been teaching the religious
Watered-down lessons
About all manner of exotic positions
He and they can't yet try
For themselves.

They simply aren't Flexible enough.

Most just borrow words
From the saints,

From those who truly
Know (wink, wink)
The Lord.

For no one can hear firsthand
The tantric melody of Solomon's Song
Without summoning the courage
To undress before God.

Strange Duet

One day,
A musician was strumming his guitar,
Singing jazzy covers
Of love ballads
In the park.

This made God very happy.

Then a goose,
With nary a musical bone in its body,
Happened to fly overhead.

Forgetting himself and his destination,
The airborne passerby
Spontaneously transformed the once-solo performance
Into a strange duet,
As he circled overhead
And squawked at full volume.

This made God even happier.

Then a park ranger came along
And broke up the affair,

Growling something about "noise ordinances"

To the musician

And "public health concerns"

To the goose.

The park ranger,

Having diligently fulfilled his duties,

Got a promotion.

And God felt sad.

Music is no longer heard in that park,

Outside of studio-approved tunes

Played on ear buds

To a thousand audiences of one.

All other unfamiliar, unpredictable

Symphonic expressions

Have been duly halted

By the appropriate authorities.

Everything is safe and orderly now.

And God feels very sad.

My Wonderful Dilemma

May I speak to you

Like we are close,

Like we are old,

Time-tested friends?

May I fast-forward

Beyond the preambles,

The tepid pleasantries,

The opening credits?

May I be so bold,

So utterly presumptuous,

As to whisper sweet nothings in your ear,

Though we've only just met?

You must pardon this silly,

Reckless heart of mine,

For it fell in love with your charms

Before you even finished

Saying your name.

Here's my wonderful dilemma:

Ever since God so tenderly removed
All the scabs from this
Soft, punctured heart,
It couldn't help but return to form,

Couldn't help but throw itself
At this wild, throbbing world.

So,

May I jump the gun
And, even now, call you by pet names
Like sweetheart, baby,
Honey, and darling?

Why not let us speak
In such intimate terms,
When my heart has already,
So thoroughly,
Given itself to you?

On the Loose

The human soul is like this—

Whenever even one feels safe enough
To finally let down its defenses
And start to unfurl,

A thousand angels lose their minds,
Frantically sounding alarm bells to indicate
It's time for heaven's residents
To don their emergency protocol sunglasses
And apply copious amounts of SPF 1 million
To every exposed limb, posthaste.

The news quickly spreads,
And ten thousand more angels start shouting
Helter-skelter in every direction,

"Everyone look out!
The Radiance of God
Is only moments away
From being on the loose!"

Abacus

God threw out
Her abacus
Long ago.

We are free
To stop counting
Too.

Smiling Through Tears

I once was told
That angels usually inhabit heaven,
Where, by the way, no tears are allowed.

It makes sense, then,
That they'd want to spend
At least some of their time down here,
Where tears are not only permitted
But wash away pain.

Angels, too, have lost friends and lovers.
Angels, too, know pain.

Too bad their motherland is ruled
By that damned Autocrat
Who demands nothing but psychotic grins
And manic clapping
And infinite hallelujahs.

But sometimes I wonder
If I was told wrong.

I wonder if the rain

Might actually be
God's precious tears.

I know that sounds silly
Coming out of the mouth
Of a full-grown man like me,
But I can't completely shake certain images
Embedded in my early psyche.

I was a child, yes, but God and I
Did happen upon one another
From time to time.

And though She always
Greeted me with a smile,
It was always that kind
Made through wet eyes
And pink-speckled cheeks,

Like when a toddler unexpectedly
Catches his mother crying.

She wipes away her tears and says,
With somehow enhanced tenderness,
"Hi baby, what is it that you need?"

Yes, that's how God smiled at me back then.

Is that how She's smiling at me now?

Smiling through tears?

I think so.

I think I was told wrong
About heaven,
About God.

Maybe angels visit Earth
For other reasons.

Contact

Psalm 136 (Richard's Version)

Give thanks to the LORD, for she is compulsive.

Her love can't help but shine.

Give thanks to the God who is addicted to compassion.

Her love can't help but shine.

Give thanks to the One who is as beholden to her nature as you and I are to ours:

Her love can't help but shine.

to she who inhabits every subatomic particle,

Her love can't help but shine.

who flirts with me uniquely in each morning's sunrise,

Her love can't help but shine.

who greets me with a dozen puppy-dog-spinnies every time I come home (props to our Maltipoo Zeta), even if I've been gone no longer than thirty seconds,

Her love can't help but shine.

who winks at me through innumerable irreverent moments and thoughts each and every day,

Her love can't help but shine.

who laughs with me at the silliness of it all,

Her love can't help but shine.

who gives me bombastic, criminal side-eye when we see people taking themselves way too seriously (and when we find ourselves doing so too),

Her love can't help but shine

who melts my heart through my youngest daughter's adoring gaze,

Her love can't help but shine.

who communes with me in my eldest daughter's listening presence,

Her love can't help but shine.

who teaches me through my son what it looks like to throw oneself at life,

Her love can't help but shine.

whose acceptance of me is mediated by my spiritual director, contemplative colleagues, spiritual direction supervisor, and a growing band of second-half misfits,

Her love can't help but shine.

whose ravenous desire for intimacy and union is mediated by my equally ravenous wife,

Her love can't help but shine.

and whose meekness is revealed in my wife's utter lack of pretense,

Her love can't help but shine.

who was brave enough to risk inviting the liquefaction of my first-half spirituality,

Her love can't help but shine.

who plays with me in Rumi's tender verses, inspires me in Mary Oliver's, frightens me in Anne Sexton's, enchants me in Daniel Ladinsky's, and seduces me in those of Hafiz,

Her love can't help but shine.

Give thanks to the God of heaven—no, strike that—to the God of Earth, to the God who emanates from materiality, from all the stuff of *this* world, to the God who can't seem to decide whether she is spiritual or physical,

    Her love can't help but shine.

The Best Unsolicited Advice You'll Ever Get

Sorrow is not your enemy.

Nor is sadness

Or grief.

Here's the best unsolicited advice you'll ever get:

Treat these banished ones

As the friends they've always longed

To be for you.

Listen to them.

Welcome them home.

Hold their shivering bodies against

The warmth of your heart's fire.

For as they melt,

They'll fill your soul's

Every fracture and fissure

With glowing, molten darkness.

Though it may sound hard to believe,

They'll somehow

Make you

Whole.

A Lament for When Dad Was Diagnosed

You were like God to me,
Invincible, unbreakable, all-problems-solvable.

What could you not do?
What could you not fix?
What gloomy day could you not brighten?

But now it's you that needs the fixing,
And I'm not sure there's anyone up to the task.

Who's great enough to fix the fixer?
How does the world make sense
When the one who's like God
Needs another who's even more like God?
How do I muster the courage to face the day
When my invincible one is no longer so?

I am exposed to the storm.
I am without a shield as arrows rain down.
I am naked in subzero temperatures.
I am the earth without its ozone.
With poles demagnetized,
Solar flares ravage my bare, delicate skin.

You were like God to me,

So what do I do now that you've been

Brought down to Earth?

Do I become God for you?

Do we become God for each other?

Are we up to the task?

Today I'm not so sure.

Maybe tomorrow I will be.

I'll just hold the paradox for now—

Frightened that you're a man after all,

But sensing that maybe, just maybe,

You're offering more of God to me now

Than ever before.

A Lament for Organization-inflicted Ouches

They love me, they love me not.
They love me, they love me not.

I serve their agenda: they love me.
I rest: they love me not.

I affirm their narrative: they love me.
I ask a question: they love me not.

I vanquish the foe: they love me.
I suffer defeat: they love me not.

I present my persona: they love me.
I muster the courage to show my true face: they love me not.

I'm overseas: they love me.
I'm home: they love me not.

I fork over my 9% assessment: they love me.
I become an inconvenience: they love me not.

I sing in unison: they love me.
I try a little harmony: they love me not.

I bind my feet like a geisha: they love me.

I "wild my feet" like a hippie: they love me not.

I make them feel good about themselves: they love me.

I rock the boat: they love me not.

I stay the same: they love me.

I grow: they love me not.

Selah.

If this is how your children treat each other, God, I'd hate to see how the reprobates behave.

But wait, I've met those reprobates. No, I've lived among them. I never affirmed Muhammad's narrative, but I couldn't get him to stop trying to hold my hand as we walked down the road. I don't remember giving Rafik 9% of anything, and now I've gone and lost track of how many times he's made me dinner. Samir doesn't seem to mind what country I'm in: I'm greeted by a WhatsApp message from him when I wake up each morning either way.

Does it bother you, Lord, that I never quite learned what conditional love looked like until I crossed paths with your zealous ones? Something seems off about that.

There was a time when they loved me. But now they love me not. There was a time when I couldn't keep up with the invitations and requests. *Come train us here. Come speak there. Come inspire us. Come tell us the stories we want to hear. Come make us feel like we haven't wasted our lives playing the roles we've played: convince us that it's all had a healthy return on investment.*

But nowadays, the phone doesn't ring as much as it used to. In fact, I can't remember the last time anyone called.

Wait ... I take that back.

Muhammad called yesterday. Rafik the day before.

I suppose I'll have to satisfy myself with being loved by them, by those who don't yet possess the good sense to make their acceptance of me conditional, by those silly, dangerous reprobates who love me without any "they love me not."

A Lament for How I've Treated My Body

You are good, but I've called you bad.
I'm so sorry for that.

Mom stood in front of the mirror and wordlessly passed
the verdict: fat, out of shape, ugly, undesirable.

Her eyes did the talking,
shouted the message back through the mirror.

I plucked out her eyes, gouged my own,
and pushing aside the tender, pulsating gore,
performed the transplant.

The gaze of disapproval now my own.

I was five.
Days, that is, not years.

The transplant performed so early it almost feels like
these are the only eyes I've ever looked through.

They might as well have been.
They have screamed the same message ever since.

Like on a pistol,
I installed a silencer to muffle their discharge,
but the bullets came out with no less frequency.
The speeding, heated lead was quieter, stealthier,
but no less damaging.

I am now almost forty-five and riddled with holes.
Swiss cheese has nothing on me.
I am more gaps than substance.
There ain't much to me left.

I can't undo forty-five years in this moment.
But I can say I'm sorry.
And I can long for a different relationship.
I can long to gaze on you with approval.
I can long to send you the messages
you've always hoped to receive.

That you are good.
That I approve of you.
That I'm glad you are mine.

That I'm glad to be with you,
right here, right now.

Come, Mother, let's stand in front of the mirror again,
let's jump on the scale once more,
but this time,

let's try shouting something new to the heavens,
and more importantly, to ourselves:

We approve!

A Lament for Betrayal

Mystery, you Who own my heart,

Betrayal sucks, and it appears to be my turn to experience its suckage. Perhaps it'll be cathartic to put words to what this has been like for me.

It's as though I've been put on trial by children, by those who are convinced their kindergarten diplomas mark the pinnacle of higher education, unable to conceive of complexities beyond crayons, construction paper, and Play-Doh. Those who regard wisdom as foolishness have appointed themselves my judges, and some idiot prankster has given them real-life robes and gavels. Those who know nothing of my soul are called as lead witnesses against me.

I am misunderstood by those who *cannot* understand. I speak a heavenly tongue, which You have taught me, but since they are unable to interpret my utterances, I'm labeled a heretic. They claim their mother tongue is God's only language, and You, O LORD, roll on the floor laughing, before whispering sweet nothings into my ear in innumerable erotic dialects.

I am a butterfly whose transformation has sent the caterpillars around me into a tizzy. They weaponize themselves with tiny scissors in hopes of clipping my wings.

They warn their children never to glance at the skies. "God wants us to forever bury our faces in milkweed," they say. They burn every chrysalis they can find.

I am a student whose experience has transcended that of his teacher and is promptly relegated to the dunce's stool for daring to speak of what he has seen and heard.

How long will light be called darkness? How long will the underdeveloped be permitted to defame the transformed? How long will the very grace of God be called evil, and growth, sin? How long will toddlers run the courtroom?

Come to my defense, O God! Let not those with no eyes call me blind. Let not those with no ears call me deaf. Draw them into the open fields in which You and I play, and laugh, and make love. Let your shameless *agape* scandalize them into submission. Let your unoffendableness melt all the offenses they take, unsolicited, on your behalf. Shock them by sending each and every one into their own chrysalis. Liquefy them. Then turn them into butterflies too, that we may laugh, soar, and play tag in the clouds together.

Either that or squash them and their little pupae under the heel of your heavenly cowboy boot. That's how psalms are supposed to go, I think.

Anyway, betrayal, am I right?

Amen.

A Lament for a Life-giving Season Drawing to a Close

It was a sweet time.
More than just a couple years to be a student,
absorbing living waters like a sponge.
The accent was on receiving,
an act that carries very little pressure with it.
To be a student is to be in the audience, not on the stage,
and to be relieved of the duty of performing
was more than a gift.
My ego had been (is still?)
addicted to being the one up front.
Endless pressure was the price to pay
for the fleeting sense of significance it offered.
It was exhausting.

Being a student gave me space to breathe.
It yanked me off the hamster wheel,
gave me permission to take a break
from the old, well-established patterns.

But now my days as a student are drawing to a close,
and I'm a bit sick to my stomach at the sense of
responsibility I feel bearing down on me.

I feel obligated to make a living
from what I've spent so long studying.
I am compulsive in passing along what I've learned.

But when I'm back "on stage,"
in the role of teacher, instructor,
wannabe sage, elder, or guru,
something doesn't feel right.
An unfreedom still has its claws sunk into my back.
My jaw clenches; my teeth grind.
My body shakes and quivers, like an impala
after having been chased by a predator.

Am I Jung's twenty-year-old,
kicking against the goads of responsibility?
Maybe, but why not let it be my turn to resist?
I haven't given myself permission before.

Why not long for the good ol' days?
Why not shirk responsibility
and revert to a less mature stage?
Why not give myself permission to fail?

We all know I won't be able to do so
for more than a microsecond,

but what a therapeutic microsecond it'll be!

Yes, God!—put on your psychotherapist's hat
and make space on your sofa for me.

I want to resist taking responsibility for a while.
I want to *not* have my act together for a moment or two,
for once in this ridiculous life of mine.

Okay, let the therapy sesh begin.

Poems by Garrison Foxwaters

A Lament for My Mom

Watching you sing "Via Dolorosa," with all the emotion
and annunciation. Your body shaking with the soprano
echoing through our humble church. The sweat running
down your neck. The intensity in your eyes, willing the
congregation to hear you. The anxious emotion of speaking
to the audience before the song, when you weren't allowed
to speak. The rejection, as music specials became a fad.

I sit here on stage with you, holding your feet, then
your knees, then your quaking arms, and finally your neck
and head. I'm gazing into your eyes while you sing one of
countless Sandi Patty songs. You held so much pain,
rejection, and loss over the years. I can feel it in your tense
body. The brokenness of your mom and dad's relationship.
The pain of dad's ineffectual love. You were sick for so
many years. The way you worked so hard at jobs and took
them so seriously, even though you weren't taken seriously.
Everything you did was intense — always so serious. I don't
know if I ever remember you in a moment of unfettered
joy. You buried pain to keep moving forward, and it killed
you, didn't it?

It seemed like there were so many ways Jeremy, Anne,
and I disappointed you. You wore that disappointment, you
prayed into it, you counseled us on it, you tried to preach
the Devil out of us. Your Bible, with its haunting black worn
cover, thick with notes, and scribbled with your meticulous
handwriting on every page. You had so much to say — to

God and everyone else. You were born into the wrong church tradition, weren't you? You were probably so frustrated and restricted in using your true gifts of teaching and prophecy that you were literally squeezing out of the edges of the tiny box those Oklahoma Baptists put you in.

Looking back today, I realize how painful that must have been. I'm so sorry, Mom. I lament what it must have been like to be in your skin. To be crushed into a little southern-Baptist-woman box over those years. To never be drawn out. Never be asked to participate. You were a born leader and disqualified at birth. Given what I have been invited to be and do as a leader and considering how my life might have been as a woman in that era, I offer you compassion I never had in my first half of life. The pressure you felt, and the pressure you put on yourself to be excellent, which turned into perfection for yourself and the expectation of perfection for us kids to become who you were never allowed the chance to become. It never made sense before now.

I'm letting go of the pain you caused me, Mom. I forgive you, and I instead hold onto some special moments when the real Dolores peeked through those clouds. Jeremy playing the guitar at Christmas and singing carols in the early '80s. The moon on the patio that night when I saw you smile. The joy Aaron brought you as a baby. The yearning to pull out the ventilator when I showed you Lila's ultrasound pictures a day before you died. I couldn't have written this in my early 20s when you were alive to read it. I grieve that you probably never felt empathy, never knew what it feels like to be understood. I offer this lament today to set us both free. I wonder about a new relationship one day on the other side. I love you, Mom.

———— .... ————

Where Are the Elders

Where are the elders?

Those weathered by the storms, beaten by the blasts,
    marked by the battles?

Those who have been born, have died and been buried,
    then reborn again, fearful and fearless for another
    round of the same,

Heavens and hells marking their journey, like tattoos on the
    back of a gang member?

All I see are the bitter, the ideological, and the triumphant
    — hardly a tattoo in sight.

Where are the elders?

Those who acknowledge the vessel that carried them to
    "here," then let it go?

Salutes drop as that ship disappears into the deep.

They look awkward with grey hair and an oar in their hand,
    sitting in a rickety canoe, where once they pushed a
    throttle and commanded a ship.

They realized at some point that original ship wasn't really
    sea-worthy, at least not for the odyssey they were being
    called to.

They were the hero in their story, until they made a hero
    for another bigger story, who may become a villain in
    our shared story if they don't sink their ship too.

Where are the elders?

Whose ears have tuned into the interior world and can offer an uncompromising listen to a youngling?

Whose self-awareness allows them to turn off their microphone and waste some time with a sojourner?

Whose life is their message?

Instead of hashtags — scars.

In place of badges of courage — dark-night tales.

In exchange for certainty — companionship.

Where are the elders?

I have met very few.

Doubt that makes them credible.

Limp that makes them approachable.

Pace that is sustainable.

Where are the elders?

Fully present, but living for a century from now?

They reveal their maturity by showing up like a child.

Elders infuriate us, inspire us, rebuke us, support us ... so, where are the elders?

———— .... ————

Garrison Foxwaters

The Myth of Garrison

The myth of Garrison is a journey of exceptionalism.

Capacity for days, multi-tasking energy, but not perfectionism.

Built for the road, military-hardened.

Beautiful feet, journey-swollen.

You've probably heard him say,

"Put me on the front line, I'm battle tested."

"I baptize you in the blood and sweat of the lost."

"Tip of the spear into the heart of darkness."

"Vegas ... Moradabad ... Nizamuddin — gates of hell, watch out!"

Normals want heroes to absolve them, undeterred.

Sheep want a cowboy who can lasso the moon and wrangle the future.

Fans want a quarterback's shirt dripping with blood.

Followers want solutions by fixers under the hood.

Teams call for leaders, sleepless, who never play hooky.

Organizations bet on their winning horse with or without a bookie.

But leadership doesn't come with warning labels.

Time management, human pace, and balance, all childhood fables.

What do you say when your daughter tells you she's never seen you cry?

How do you sleep with that relentless, "Why?"

The myth of Garrison isn't a unique story.

Heroic leadership is a familiar glory.

Intoxicating possibility-ing,

soul-crushing scheduling,

enemies on all sides, pouncing,

interior life crumbling,

unflappable facade reinforcing,

family-, role-, support-juggling,

caffeine-induced marching,

speed-limit never-driving,

keep the drumbeat high so you can't hear the demons taunting.

"Was I made for this, or did I make this?"

"Who is in my wake, will they become 'this'?"

Garrison's disciples dauntless,

but 100 years from now, what will be left?

———— .... ————

Burn

In my youth, I wanted to be consumed by the fire of God,

My lust for everything and everyone — I knew if I could,
I'd make love to the whole world.

Terrifying hunger.

I feared how much power I felt inside me, how fearless I
was.

"Lord, burn it up, burn it all!"

In my thirties, I wanted God's fire for a different
consuming.

My ambition and lust for power were intoxicating and most
everyone thought I should wield it, so I did.

And the wake of my leadership was a wildfire for everyone
around me.

"Lord, burn it up, burn it all!"

In my forties, I wanted yet another kind of consuming fire
of God.

I've been in the room where it happens. When the tension
of holding space for hundreds who lead thousands
breaks the back and leaves the seasoned speechless.

When the pressure to offer certainty and safety foiled faith
and made me question my own.

"Lord, burn it up, burn it all!"

Today, coming into my fifties, I don't think I want to be consumed by God's fire anymore.

I want to join God as fire.

I want to be revealed as an element, indestructible.

I want to be refined in an encounter that includes all the mysterious parts of us both.

I want who I am in all its elementality to be fused in a white-hot union with God the way my early theology couldn't comprehend.

I sense the invitation to shift from being an object in a sentence others write about God and Garrison to joining God in the subject and co-creating the object.

Or maybe it's unleashing the co-creation everywhere with everyone who feels they are a mere "log in the fire."

Now, metaphor becomes me.

I am a container for the fire of those who consider themselves wood and want to be consumed.

I am the fire as an image-bearer and co-incendiary — consuming, refining, revealing, enduring.

And ... I am mysteriously also the wood as I sit bedazzled by the flames and warmed by my fire on a chilly November morning.

"... burn it up, burn it all!"

———— .... ————

Garrison Foxwaters

Poems by Yusuf Ishqzoda

The Prestige

I volunteered, and the assistant took my hand as I stepped
onto the stage.

Rabbits. Swords. Glass prisons were pushed to the back as
the game was introduced.

Today's game was hide and seek.
I was to search. She was to hide.

She disappeared, and the crowd gasped.

Delight! The search was on.

In the large chest? Empty!

In the stage closet? Nothing!

Crowd members turned to the right, left.
Above. Below. Murmurs started.

"What kind of joke is this?"
"We paid good money for this?"
"Do something, fool! She's waiting on you."

"You've messed it up!"

I begin to pace. I go backstage. Costumes.
    Contraptions. Connivings.
    But she is nowhere.

Back to the stage, and the room is emptying.
    Her assistant offers me the keys.
    "Lock up when you leave."

The door slams. The lights drop.
    I am alone.

And that's when she unveils.

———— .... ————

Yusuf Ishqzoda

Prestige (Part 2)

You are no two-bit
Magician with a second
rabbit under the table
to pull out of the hat.

You hide greater things
with love, purpose, meaning,
and place them under
the veil of violence, grief,
cancer.

Does not the scope of a
magician's stage intensify
the shock, the hope of
the reveal? When the crowd
assumes the death of the
underwater assistant, is the joy
in her life not greater?

Or is that just a cheap trick
to feed our adrenaline
with the rush of another's
suffering?

I'm not sure.

———— .... ————

Yusuf Ishqzoda

Some Days

Some days,

    I hoot and holler in praise

        of the artist

            who writes a masterpiece

        in which he bears

            the crux

    of   the   plot.

Some days

    I revolt against

        the seedy details

            of the script,

      and closing the book,

        I search for the

            censor's pyre.

—— .... ——

Yusuf Ishqzoda

What If

What if life were really
  just an ongoing conversation
  with You?

What if other people, lovers, enemies,
  events, tragedies, celebrations, everything
    and everyone
      were never an interruption
  but a twist,
    a turn,
      a deepening,
        a joke
    to spice up
      our discussion?

What if life were really
  just an ongoing dance
    with You?

Indeed.

What if everyone was really
  part of the dance, knowingly

or not?

We line dance with

the inspired.

We bump into

those standing still.

We collide with

those going the other way.

It all makes the dance

interesting,

unsettling,

surprising,

seductive.

They liven the rhythm,

innovate,

upend,

create.

Mmmmm.

Let's just drop the what-if.

—— .... ——

Yusuf Ishqzoda

Sans Invitation

Vocatus atque non vocatus,
Deus aderit.

God is
The great
Party Crasher.

So save your breath,
Maybe even a tree,

For he loves
Making his appearance
Sans invitation.

Truth Be Told

When's the last time
You teased God
About something?

Truth be told:

He gets tired of all our reverence sometimes,
Tired of all that insists on distance
Between our souls
And his.

When's the last time
You razzed the Lord
For one of his many quirks?

Truth be told:

All he really wants are a few close friends,
A few loved ones intimate enough
To poke fun at him
From time to time.

Spirit Animal

What is your spirit animal?

I think mine might be
The mongoose.

I, too, have made meals
Out of Dangerous Things.

The snakes of
Doubt,
Darkness,
Irreverence,
And all manner of serpents profane,

On these I have dined.

Yes,
I must be a
Spiritual Mongoose.

I eat darkness and doubt—
Ingest the sacred seed—

And give birth to God.

On Mystics and Religions

A wise man
Once said,

"A kite with no string
Is only fun
For so long,

But a string with no kite
Is no fun
At all."

In the Mighty Name of Jesus

God is too wild,
Too unpredictable,
Too mysterious,
Too playful,
Too shameless,
For our frightened species
To long tolerate.

That's why,
In the mighty name of Jesus,
We surround him with
Countless yards
Of caution tape.

That's why,
In the holy name of Jesus,
We quarantine God.

An Angel Told Me

The other day,
An angel told me about
A scene that plays out
All too often
In heaven.

A near-perfect person of faith
Makes his or her arrival
And approaches the Christ,
Beaming,

"It worked!
Hallelujah, it worked!

I paid heed to all the warnings,
Steered clear of all contaminants.

I avoided public education,
Took in no secular media.

Treated the R rating like the plague,
Emerged victorious in the battle with lust.

Tuned out evolution's deceptions,
Ignored science in its entirety.

I even made the Hajj to the Creation Museum,
Safely situated in Kentucky consecrated.

I did it!
I adhered to each and every prohibition!
I kept the World away!"

And that's when the Christ extends his hand—
A tear rolling down his earth-stained cheek—

And says,

"Hi, my name is Jesus,
It's very nice to meet you."

Hafiz

Give it a try, you say?
Very well.

If someone passes by
And our eyes meet,

If my glance does not warm their soul,
If it does not make them blush
As I drink in their loveliness,

Then, Richard,
Quickly run to the basilica and pray—

For you have just committed
The only sin I know.[1]

Untangle This Riddle

Let's see if you can
Untangle this riddle:

There is no better way
To summarize development
Than to say that
The subject of one stage
Becomes the object of the subject
Of the next stage.[2]

Once decoded, these words
Make plain what Jesus meant
When he told me,

"There's no question
That saddens me more
Than, 'Is it biblical?'"

Something I Love About God

One

Of the

Things I love

About the

Friend

Is

How every

Time I stumble

Upon one

Of

Her

Devilishly creative

Hiding spots I

Always find

Her

Smiling.

Climax

Then the Penny Dropped

I used to think
I sounded very intelligent
Every time I pointed out:

"We're talking about
Two sides of
The same coin."

Then the penny dropped,
And now I know:

It's a one-sided coin.

How Sweet the Day

How sweet the day
When my soul first dared
To accept that it is accepted.

And how much sweeter the day
When the Friend first revealed
That deeper, more sacred truth:

That acceptance and unacceptance,
In-ness and out-ness,
Aren't even categories

In this Reality
Whose name is

One.

Knock, Knock

Want to hear a joke?

Sure.

Knock, knock.

Who's there?

Two.

A Humble Suggestion

The Beloved and I have

A humble suggestion

For all temples,

Synagogues,

Mosques,

Churches,

Et cetera.

Given that all language

Has taken an oath

To fail to describe Him,[3]

We recommend dedicating half—

Make it three-quarters—

Of every worship service

To maintaining unadulterated

Silence.

You know what?

That gives me an idea.

That Point Being Made

That point being made,
Words sure are fun.

In fact, allow me to clear my conscience
And confess that they and I have been having
A torrid love affair for longer than
I can remember.

Having gotten that off my chest,
Back to the point at hand.

It is in the name of Fun
That the Beloved and I
Can't help but co-recommend
Your religious gatherings remain
At least twenty-five percent comprised
Of all that language-sourced,
Unwarranted confidence-drenched,
Wildly humorous
Sacrilege.

If Things Go Well

You don't show up naked for the date.

It begins with getting all dolled up,

With learning to slip into that most tantalizing dress,
To get every cuff link situated
On that most flattering, form-fitting suit.

In technical terms,
This is the stage of getting
One's shit together.

And if things go well,
It eventually all falls apart.

The dress gets snagged on a ragged edge
And is torn beyond repair.

The form-fitting suit no longer fits the form.
The word "flattering" no longer applies.

The dress,
The suit,

They end up crumpled in a pile on the floor.

And if things go *really* well ...

Do I really need to explain the fun that can be had
Once you're down to your birthday suit?

Things Are Much Better Now

I used to be a very serious person.

That was before the deepest regions of my soul,
Along with some great saints,
Gave me permission to stop believing
Ideas about God that made me sad.

Things are much better now.

Whispering

Shouting is for the certain,
Or those who would like to be.

But whispering and silence,
Those are for lovers.

I used to shout a lot,
Even traveling to distant lands
To do so.

Not so much anymore.

There's simply too much whispering
Going on between God and I
These days.

Sprinting Between Chairs

I've been starting to think
The Bible might be onto something
When it speaks of Jesus as our advocate,

But I also think we get just about
Everything else in the metaphor
Wrong from there.

Enlightenment, from this perspective,
Could very well be
Awakening to the reality
That the heavenly courtroom
Would be otherwise unoccupied
Were it not for our tragic compulsion
To sprint between chairs,
Alternating among the roles of
Judge, jury, and lead prosecutor
In our own self-convened trials.

And there stands Jesus, our advocate,
Confessing,

"To be honest, I often feel uncomfortable

Spending so much time in a setting
So foreign to my nature,"

Before stomping his foot and saying,

"But I'll be damned
If I'm going to let you
Pass the verdict 'bad'
On a Miracle my Father
So clearly regards as good."

Stop the Presses

I once asked God,
"Is every good and perfect gift
Really from you?"

"Yes," she said,
"But not just *from* me,
Are me."

"What about everything else?"
I then inquired.

And leaning in, she responded
In a playfully hushed tone,
"I'll let you in on a secret.
I really *am* love,
And love never wars,
Never divides,
Which means I don't know
How to push a single thing away.
So, yes, *all* is me."

"Only one more then," I dared venture,
"What about separation and union themselves?"

And God broke out in Laughter,
Bellowing,

"Stop the presses,
You're really getting it now!

You caught me, my friend,
Both am I."

What Else Can I Conclude

Have you ever had the feeling
That this thing called existence
Is, at its core, an enormous setup
For some grand divine punchline,

And that God is barely able
To restrain his good-hearted laughter
As he struggles to retell a joke he once heard
At some splendid celestial dinner party?

What else can I conclude,
When I keep running into
So many mini-punchlines
Along the way,

When God's humor,
Both light and dark,
Is so clearly present in
Everything I see, taste, and touch?

Defining Sin

There is a waist-high container
With two halves to it.

The container itself is labeled "Either-Or."

On one half, in smaller font,
The word "Good" is written—
On the other half, "Bad."

This "Either-Or" container,
Soundly constructed though it is,
Does not stand alone.

It lives happily
Within a much larger container
Labeled "Both-And."

Try drawing this image in the space below.

Now to the topic of sin.

Sin is everything that follows

Once an eviction notice

Has been served

To "Either-Or."

Wouldn't It Be Silly

Imagine getting your hands
On a great novel—
Let's say one of Tolstoy's,
Or Dostoyevsky's,
Or (insert your favorite novelist here),

But as you thumb through
Its pages for the first time,
A particular footnote
Catches your attention,

And you become so fixated
On this footnote that you
Forget to read the novel itself,

Becoming so lost in the weeds, in fact,
That you mistake the footnote for
The novel's main plot.

Wouldn't it be silly to do that?
...
Wouldn't it?
...

American Evangelicalism,

Wouldn't it?

God Meant It

There are three perspectives
That won't serve you well in life:

I am bad.
The world is bad.
The future is bad.

For many of us,
The most arduous leg
Of the spiritual journey
Involves the painstaking process
Of unlearning these lies.

Some never break free.

Some even wed these abusers,
Unable to imagine life without them.

But I'll tell you this:

God meant it,
O, she *really* meant it,

When she called
This world, its creatures,
And its future

Good and *Very Good.*

Afterglow

My Other Spirit Animal

I once said that my spirit animal
Must be the mongoose,
And that remains true.

But it struck me the other day
That I probably have another,
Given that most important things in life
Are best expressed by paradox.

So let's say I'm both a mongoose
And a panda.

Beyond sharing a certain,
Shall I say, rotundness,
We each have become somehow utterly
Convinced that our natural habitats
Are rather jolly, safe places—

The bamboo forest for them,
The ocean of God for me—

And therefore busy ourselves,
Not with setting up defenses against threats,

But with curiously exploring our terrains,

Stumbling carefree from grace to grace,

And taking frequent extended breaks

To refine our practice of the twin spiritual disciplines of

Snacking and Lounging.

I don't know about pandas,

But in my case, the blame for

This outright obliviousness to danger

Absolutely must be placed on God.

He has treated me, you see,

So kindly for so long

That I've simply lost track of any reason

Why I should be afraid of him.

Odd Man Out

"We are but clods of earth,"
Opined the elderly guru to his
Breathless, enraptured audience,

And as if on cue,
Everyone grunted solemn approval
And began searching in earnest
For mischievous pens that always seem to be winning
Unannounced games of hide-and-seek
To jot this quotation down in journals
Of varying price points and elegance.

Everyone except for this odd man out.

It seems I was the only one in the room
Who found our guru's put-down
To be a strange way to remind us
Of our supposed lowliness,

As if stardust congealed into such
Spectacular form could do anything
But confront me with my own grandeur,

As if the literal one in seventy trillion
Genetic miracle that is Richard H. Barry—

That is each one of us—

Could lead me to grunt anything other than
The dissenting, worshipful words,

"Clods of earth, my ass!"

God's Puckered Lips

Wayfarer,

Has no one ever told you

That this World

Is nothing other than

God's puckered lips?

I implore you, burdened friend:

Don't let another day go by

Without snagging at least a few

Big wet smooches!

Have a Seat

Two things experience has taught me:

One, I tend to take myself too seriously,
And, two, God has a way of, shall we say,
Deflating tensions.

Right when I'm most rattled,
Most worked into a tizzy,

Right when my vision is most obscured
By anxiety, offense, indignation, or self-contempt,

Right when I've reached drop-dead serious mode,

God sneaks his Whoopee Cushion
Into the moment
And invites me to
Have a seat.

Eyes to See

Don't worry, dear one:
I have eyes to see.

Eyes to see in you
What many have missed,
And what many more
Have misunderstood.

Eyes to see the beautiful creature
Taking shape in your inmost sanctum's
Holy, fertile Darkness.

Take heart, beloved of God:
Your impregnation was his doing.

Have patience, treasured of God:
Your soul's gestation cannot be hurried.

And make no mistake,
This new life is no abomination.

Quite the opposite.

It is Christ in you,
The hope of glory.

It is losing your whole world
Yet gaining your soul.

It is you, at long last,
Selling everything you own
For the pearl of great price
Buried at your core.

Yes, I see the beautiful creature
Forming in your depths.

May our friendship bring this
Divine pregnancy to term.

May it become both
Incubator and midwife
For the wild, precious Gift
That is, even at this moment,
Kicking your belly from within.

Imagine a Girl

It seems I'm not quite done
Making a certain point,

So let's try another approach.

Imagine a girl,
Born and raised
On a remote homestead
With only her family
To keep her company.

The girl blossoms
Into a stunning beauty,
But owing to some strange, tragic
Mixture of ignorance and folly,
Her parents and siblings
Take it as their sacred duty
To bring to her attention—
With exasperating regularity—
Just how ordinary, even repulsive,
They find her appearance to be.

Even when this certifiable bombshell

One day ventures far from home,

Setting down roots in a saner

Corner of God's green earth,

Might it not take

A great deal of time

For her to recover?

Might not her self-confidence struggle,

Perhaps her whole life long,

To find its firm footing?

Her head would no doubt

Learn the truth of her beauty

Long before her gut,

Long before her bones and marrow

Had time to play catch up.

If only she could somehow grasp

Her inherent, breathtaking majesty.

If only you could too.

You see,

Like Kamala,
You were that girl.

In fact, you *are* that girl,
Convinced of your plainness,
Fed the lie of your homeliness,
Though nothing could be
Further from the truth.

And though the road to recovery
May be long, hear this now:

You are anything but ordinary!

Quarks aren't ordinary, after all—
Magical is a term far more fitting—
The same applying to the
Particles, atoms, and molecules
To which they give rise.

So,

How could an against-all-odds collection
Of sentient, self-aware molecules
Ever be considered ordinary?

How could a once-in-a-species
Expression of the Source
Be judged as plain?

How could a bipedal universe
Of longing, pain, hope, and dread
Dare be reckoned as anything other
Than an outright marvel?

You truly are that girl.

My prayer is that you will
One day unlearn the lessons
Unlearned men have taught you,

And one day come to know,
Deep in your bones,
The absolute wonder that you are.

They Can Tell

I'm sitting at Starbucks today,
Spending time with the tender verses
Of saints like Catherine of Siena,
Hafiz and Thích Nhất Hạnh.

Maybe this isn't the place
To be exposed to such
Otherworldly Kindness,

Such otherworldly Love.

I keep dropping my phone
And burying my face in my hands
In an attempt to make the employees
And customers around me feel
Slightly less uncomfortable.

It isn't working.

They can tell
Something tremendously intimate
Is taking place between me
And whoever's words I'm reading.

They can tell
Sweet nothings
Usually reserved for the bedroom
Are being whispered in a coffee shop.

That's on me.

I'll be more careful next time
Where I read the overtures of
God's holy band of courtesans.

May I Have This Dance

It isn't all bad,

This desire we have
To work, work, work
Toward some grand
Healing of this world.

It's just rather ironic.

We want to work for God,
While she just wants to dance,
Knowing that healing, without a thought,
Trails her sublime movements like a wake.

All she needs is a partner.

And there we are fretting,
Even scolding the Divine,

"You really need to
Stop all this dancing—

You know?—

And get back to work
Healing the world."

What a remarkable capacity we have
For missing the point!

So allow me to state it plainly:

It is the dance that heals.

And the look in God's eye,
Not to mention the deep breath
She just took, tells me
She's almost done mustering
The courage to ask you,

"May I have this dance?"

This One's for the Eights

The goal was to make life look effortless, to make it appear
   as though keeping my act together was a piece of cake,

To live in an eternally productive spring—no winters
   needed, no winters allowed.

As TikTok is teaching my teenage son to say today, "Light
   work, no reaction."

The most effective means of achieving this, I found, was to
   deaden myself to stimuli. I covered every square inch of
   my vulnerable, receptive body with a glossy, rubbery
   coating. I could keep moving forward uninhibited, as
   everything the world threw at me either slid or bounced
   right off.

The only price I had to pay was the forfeiture of being
   touched.

And for this I won awards.

I could mold the world around me without it ever molding
   me in return.

Blue ribbon.

I could keep pressing on in the face of a hurricane because even gale-force winds couldn't get through my rubbery armor to make landfall on my petrifying skin.

Gold star.

I could already hear the God of my ancestors forming the words, "Well done, good and faithful servant."

Selah.

"What's your secret?" some would ask. "How do you stay so unabatedly productive?"

I'd hem and I'd haw, dancing around the subject in ways I hoped sounded intelligent. What I never said, though, was the truth: "The secret to contentment in all things, zealous ones, is to never feel—or, better yet, never let yourself be touched."

Then, one day, I got tired of not being touched. I shed the protective coating. And I've since been learning firsthand how amazing and terrifying and exhilarating and dreadful a thing it is to be affected, to be impacted, to be molded, to be touched.

I don't always make life look easy anymore. And now that I mention it, the nudge to engage myself in that enterprise seems to present itself less frequently with each passing day.

In fact, some days I don't make it look easy at all, much less sophisticated. Like a whore wiping the Sacred's perfumed feet with her hair and tears, I go around touching and being touched in countless wild, awkward, transgressively intimate ways,

And I seem to be losing interest in reading the room to detect signs that I've crossed the boundaries of good decorum.

Selah.

There don't appear to be any awards coming my way for this behavior, but I'll be damned if I don't feel more alive now than ever before.

And more in love.

And that's award enough for me.

All because I allowed myself to feel.
All because I allowed myself to be touched.

Three Daves and a Gondola Ride

A trio of retiree friends
Shuffle spryly into the gondola,
And the attendant motions me,
A single rider, to join them.

The doors close,
And a mischievous look
Appears on each of their faces
Before one of the three Daves,
Each from a different town
Outside of Boston, asks,

"Mind if we smoke weed on the way up?"

"It'll be a much funner ride if we do,"
I respond, trying to give the impression
That I have more experience
With recreational cannabis
Than I actually do.

My answer seems to satisfy,
As good-spirited laughter fills
The frosty cabin,

And Dave 1 confesses,

"Well, bad news, we don't really have any,
But you can tell a lot about a person
By how they react to that question!"

A few moments later,
Names having been exchanged,
Dave 2 asks another,

"So, Richard, what do you do for a living?"

And I, once again, find myself rifling through
The Rolodex of vague, eyebrow-raising
Replies at my disposal—

Wondering anew if I'll ever be the owner
Of a simple, straightforward answer—

Before deciding to offer a response
That still feels like a half-truth, at best.

"I'm a poet," I say,
And their heads tilt in concert,
Displaying a collective curiosity.

Dave 3 jumps in,
"What kind of people read your poetry?"

"Not many," I self-effacingly admit,
"But those who do tend to appreciate
A mystical outlook on life."

The next few moments are predictably
Spent clarifying the meaning of words
Like mystical and mysticism,

Denoting a spirituality that's more interested
In detecting God's presence emanating
From this-worldly, lived experience
Than in demanding conformity
To any particular set of doctrines.

"We need more of that in this world,"

Dave 3 says while shaking his head,
Indicating that, like many poor souls,
His experience of religion has been
Something less than ideal.

The same is true for Daves 1 and 2,

One of whom hypothesizes,

"So that must be why you're
Out here on the mountain today,
To meet God on the slopes."

"Exactly," I light up,
"See, this guy gets it!"

We all chuckle,

And I think I see a momentary glint
In Dave 1's eye, hinting at a
Hope beyond hope that seems
To have snuck up on him,

A sacred intuition that the familiar act
Of gliding down a mountainside
Might have been hiding an encounter
With God all along,

And that some wonder-kissed
Segment of his soul has been wise
To this truth since time immemorial.

Dave 1 tells of his Catholic upbringing,
Of being forced to go to Mass every Sunday,

Of how he sensed by middle school
That he'd already learned everything
The church had to teach him,

And that to keep attending
Would be to expose himself
To a tireless regurgitation
Of the same old, same old.

"No, thanks," he concludes.

Dave 2 smiles broadly as he speaks
Of the scandalous union
Of his Jewish father
And Christian mother,

His smile dissipating as he recounts
Their resultant excommunication
From both sides of the family,

Religion being the sole reason
He never really knew any of

His grandparents, aunts,
Uncles, or cousins.

Dave 3 announces,

"I was raised New England Methodist,
But then I studied engineering,
And engineers can't swallow all that
'On such and such day, God made ...'
Nonsense."

We chuckle again
And spend the rest of our gondola ride
Bemoaning the foolishness of treating
Genesis like a science textbook
Rather than a creation myth
Rich in symbolism and meaning,

A book rendered limp and listless
By the misplaced demands of literalism.

All this on an eight-minute
Journey to the summit
Of Loon Mountain.

The automated doors slide open,
And Dave 1 quips,
With characteristic charm,

"Maybe you'll write a poem some day
About the three Daves who asked
If they could smoke weed with you
On a gondola ride."

"Maybe I will,"
I warmly respond,

Before bidding them adieu,
Skiing down to the lodge,
And spending the rest of the morning
Doing exactly that.

A Silly Thought

I woke up in a cold sweat
Last night, owing to a disturbing,
Most unnatural dream.

For in it, enjoying God
And enjoying the world
Were two different things,

Endeavors that even seemed
To be at odds with one another.

I know it's a silly thought,
But imagine if it were true!

Imagine the havoc we would wreak
Were we to live according to such a
Misinformed nightmare!

As for Me

As for me,
I have come
Not to bring a sword,

Nor to fulfill the law,
Destroy the works of the devil,
Or set the world on fire,

But for one reason alone:

That my eyes might tell
Every creature I meet
Just how lovely they are,

Which, now that I think of it,
Might end up setting
A few hearts on fire,

And a few captives free.

Acknowledgments

Many thanks to my teenage daughters, neither of whom considered it beneath them to intern with their old man for the sake of moving this project forward. I will write poetry until my dying day if it keeps giving me an excuse to spend time with you.

Thank you, Natalie, for designing this book's cover, as well as that of *Her Name is Mystery*. If the glory of God is a human being fully alive, then some of that glory is undoubtedly manifest in your skills and talents.

Brian and Laura, your friendship has been a source of nourishment for my soul for more than two decades. Thank you for who you are: thoughtful, irreverent, kind, generous, wildly humorous ... did I mention irreverent? As you know, this book's title was born from your vision of God. It is a beautiful vision indeed, one that most religions could use a healthy dose of.

Notes

1. Daniel Ladinsky's rendering of Hafiz is the source of the phrase "For you have just committed / The only sin I know." Daniel Ladinsky, *I Heard God Laughing: Poems of Hope and Joy—Renderings of Hafiz* (New York: Penguin Books, 2006), 56.

2. This summary of human development is influenced by Robert Kegan. Cf. Kegan, *The Evolving Self: Problem and Process in Human Development* (Cambridge, MA: Harvard University Press, 1982).

3. The words "all language has taken an oath to fail to describe Him" are borrowed from Meister Eckhart. See Daniel Ladinsky, *Love Poems from God: Twelve Sacred Voices from the East and West* (New York: Penguin Books, 2002), 97.